OPAL DUNN is a well-known specialist in early first and second language development. She acted as Chief Consultant to Linguaphone's prize-winning course, Children's English, and works as a consultant to the Council of Europe on children's bilingual education. Her books include the Match and Patch series; UNESCO'S *Let's Play Asian Children's Games*; *Mr Bear's Book of Rhymes* and *Help Your Child with a Foreign Language* (Berlitz). Her previous titles for Frances Lincoln are *Un Deux Trois – First French Rhymes*, and *Hippety-hop, Hippety-hay! – Growing with rhymes from birth to age 3*.

SUSAN WINTER was born in South Africa and graduated from Natal University, before becoming a social worker, first in South Africa and later in London. After the birth of her second child, she studied illustration at Chelsea School of Art, and began a new career as a freelance illustrator of children's books. Her previous titles include *Henry's Baby* and *The Bear That Went to Ballet* (Dorling Kindersley); *The Winchelsea Trilogy* and *The Ghost Watchers* (Hodder & Stoughton); *Nicky and the Twins* (HarperCollins) and *Calling All Toddlers* (Orion). Susan's first book for Frances Lincoln was *Copy me, Copycub* by Richard Edwards.

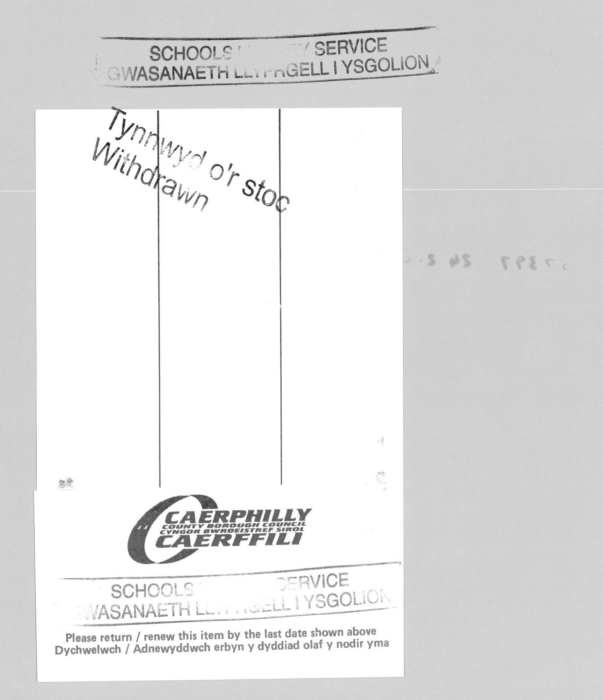

To Michael and Lily, and all the other children
around the world with whom I have had fun
playing games. – OD

To Jessica, with love. – SW

Acker Backa BOO! copyright © Frances Lincoln Limited 2000
Text copyright © Opal Dunn 2000
Illustrations copyright © Susan Winter 2000
Music arranged by Margaret Lion

First published in Great Britain in 2000 by
Frances Lincoln Limited, 4 Torriano Mews,
Torriano Avenue, London NW5 2RZ

First paperback edition 2001

British Library Cataloguing in Publication Data available on request

ISBN 0-7112-1588-X hardback
ISBN 0-7112-1662-2 paperback

Printed in Hong Kong

1 3 5 7 9 8 6 4 2

The Author, Illustrator and Publisher disclaim responsibility for any
adverse effects resulting directly or indirectly from the games and activities
described and illustrated herein, or from the reader's misunderstanding
of the text or illustrations.

The author was inspired by the works of Iona and Peter Opie and would like
to thank UNESCO and UNICEF for their co-operation, as well as
the many friends all over the world who have helped her in over 50 years
of playing and collecting games.

Acker Backa BOO!

Opal Dunn
Illustrated by Susan Winter

FRANCES LINCOLN

Contents

Note to Parents, Teachers and Carers   7

Introduction   8

Easy-Peasy Games   10

Whose Turn? Games   14

Hands and Feet Mover Games   18

Catch You Games   22

Ball Games   26

Hide and Seek Games   30

Clap, Skip and Jump Games   34

Singing Games   38

Music   42

Tips on Playing the Games   44

Index of Games and List of Countries   45

Dear Parents, Teachers and Carers,

Can you remember the excitement and fun you had playing games when you were young? Children love to play games and they will happily play a game again and again, without getting bored. Within the confines of a game, they feel secure as they know what to expect.

Games, like stories, are powerful teaching experiences. The games in *Acker Backa BOO!* are accompanied by simple rhymes, which help develop children's understanding of language and its sounds. This, in its turn, speeds up the process of learning to read – beginner readers soon discover they can read rhymes they know well. Although this is 'memory reading', it is an important step towards becoming a fluent reader, as it helps to motivate the child and build self-confidence.

Games provide many informal opportunities to teach values and attitudes. Through them you can convey concepts such as fair play, being a good loser, having courage and self-control, as well as sharing and thinking of others. Games involve decision-making as well as physical and emotional participation – as they play, children learn by doing, and at the same time they learn how to learn.

Children learn by imitating and copying, so your example in playing with them provides an important role model. Young children want to please their parents and the adults they love, and it is through seeking your positive reactions that they find out about right and wrong and what is expected of them.

My selection of games is global, because I feel it is important for children to grow up knowing that they can feel the same emotions as children in other countries and societies, and can even use some of the same language. Don't worry about using the correct pronunciation – children's playground language is rarely standard, anyway.

Games can provide a link in global understanding on which adults can build, and I hope that this book will start you off!

Have fun!

Opal Dunn

Introduction

Every game in this book has a simple rhyme or song to accompany it. Instructions for adults on how to play are also included and most games are illustrated.

Many traditional games are global: they have travelled across continents and been adapted on their way, so often their origin is unclear. The countries in which these games are played have been listed. They may be played in other countries too and some of them may already be familiar to you.

Easy-Peasy Games

These games have been selected to help children of about 3 years-old learn about games and how to play them. Children have to learn that games are different from free play. Learning about games takes time, so as you play together, keep explaining the aim and the rules. At first they might find it hard to accept that rules cannot be changed and they may try to negotiate. Learning about winners and losers can sometimes be a little painful to begin with, so make sure that, next time they play, you give them a chance to win. Once children have grasped how to play and their concentration has developed, try extending games they already know or introduce a new Easy-Peasy game.

Whose Turn? Games

These games aim to find one person to have a turn, be a catcher, or just be the winner. They provide an excellent way to make a fair decision, avoiding discussion. Counting corresponds to the beats in the rhyme and is confirmed by a tap or point of a finger.

Hands and Feet Mover Games

These games give children an opportunity to compete with themselves and each other, and to monitor their own improvement. Through games, children learn how to be honest with themselves and how to identify their weak points as well as their strengths. They find out that by sticking at something, they can improve a skill. In this way they learn to accept a challenge and face it with confidence.

Catch You Games

Children get fun and excitement from these games, as they know that the fantasy, danger and stress are confined. Through the games, they learn survival techniques, how to act heroically, and how to manage themselves in order to escape or, if they want, be caught. For many children these games are important as they provide a brief escape from the stresses and worries of their everyday life.

Ball Games

These games involve the physical skill of handling a ball. Teach the ball skill first and then introduce the game. Start with a larger ball and reduce the size as the child's skill increases. If you are worried about balls, use beanbags instead. In the early years, girls often have better ball skills than boys; they also tend to practise more by themselves.

Hide and Seek Games

Most of these games are played in the same way with a hider, a seeker and a safe home base. Children love these games and are ready to play from quite a young age, if the surroundings are familiar. Young children have to learn where and how to hide effectively and often need your advice.

Clap, Skip and Jump Games

All these games have very strong beats, which regulate the rhythm and help to keep time. When playing the skipping games, turn the rope yourself at first, as children may find this difficult. Young children find it easier to learn the actions first, then the rhyme.

Singing Games

These games can be played with children of all ages, or with the whole family on special occasions. When you introduce a game, it may be easier to begin by humming the tune and clapping to the rhythm. Once the children are confident, add the words and actions of the song. Music can be found on P42-43.

Easy-Peasy Games

Wolf, Wolf, where are you?

One child is the Wolf. The other children run up to him saying the first two lines of the rhyme. The Wolf replies with the next three lines, whilst pretending to put on his clothes. Then he shouts, "I'm COMING!" and chases the children. The first caught becomes the Wolf next time.

France, Switzerland

Andar, Bahar

The children stand inside a circle of chalk or twigs. The leader shouts "Inside – Andar", and the children jump inside the circle, or "Outside – Bahar", and they jump outside. The leader continues, getting faster and faster. If she shouts "Andar" when the children are already inside the circle, or "Bahar" when they are already outside, they must freeze. Children who do not follow the commands correctly are out.

India (Hindi)

Wolf, Wolf, where are you?
Can you hear me?
I'm putting on my pullover,
I'm putting on my trousers,
I'm putting on my socks,
I'm COMING!

Inside – Andar,
Outside – Bahar,
Andar, Bahar,
Andar, Bahar,
BAHAR.

Stroke the baby,
Stroke the baby.
Guess who did it!

I looked high
And I looked low.
Where did she put it?
I don't know.

Cross your hands,
Cross your hands,
Where is it now?

Hum a dum dum,
A finger or a thumb?

Stroke the baby

One child is the Baby and faces the wall. Another child strokes her back whilst the rest of the group say the rhyme. The child facing the wall then turns around and tries to guess who stroked her back. If she guesses right, that child becomes the Baby. If not, she has another turn.

UK

I looked high

One child hides a soft toy as the others count to 5 with their eyes shut. While they search for it, they say the rhyme. The finder hides the toy next time.

Australia, Canada, UK, USA

Cross your hands

One child shows the group a small object, then hides it in one fist, behind his back. Next, he crosses his hands in front of him as the group says the rhyme. He then asks a member of the group to guess in which hand the object is hidden.

Sri Lanka

Hum a dum dum

One child hides his face in his lap. Another child taps him on the shoulder as she says the rhyme, and ends by holding up a finger or a thumb. The first child then guesses which she is holding up. If he guesses right, he says the rhyme next time.

UK

13

Whose Turn? Games

Acker backa boo!
Count between two children or round a group, pointing to a new child with each word. Eliminate the child you are pointing to as you say "YOU". The last child left in the game wins.

Canada, UK, USA

Olika bolika
Count the feet of children sitting in a circle as you say each word of the rhyme. The child whose foot you are pointing to on "NOB" should bend his knee and tuck his foot under him. The last child with a foot still sticking out, wins.

Belgium, Germany, Holland, UK

Acker Backa Soda Cracker,
Acker Backa Boo!
Acker Backa Soda Cracker,
Out Goes YOU.

Olika bolika,
Susan solika,
Olika bolika,
NOB.

Tickum-tackum,
Tickum-tackum,
Tickum-tackum,
MORE.

Up and down,
Up and down,
Up and down,
And STOP.

Ram, ram,
Ram, ram,
Ram, ram,
RIP.

Tickum-tackum

Two players walk 3 metres apart, shout "tickum-tackum" and turn round. They then take turns walking forward, putting heel to toe, the first player shouting "tickum" and the second player "tackum" as they go. The child whose foot fills the final gap is the winner.

Iran, UK

Up and down

Three or more players hold hands and swing them up and down. On the word "STOP", they place their right hand on their left hand, either palm up or palm down. If there are more palms *up* than *down*, the palms *down* win, and vice versa. Play continues among the winners until there is one child left. (If 2 children are left, then the game is replayed from the beginning.)

Pakistan

Ram, ram, RIP

One player holds out his hand, palm up. The others rest the tips of their first fingers on his palm. The first player says the rhyme, and on "RIP", he closes his hand quickly and tries to catch a finger. The player whose finger is caught is out. If he catches more than one, the game is played again.

Indonesia, Malaysia

Hands and Feet Mover Games

Bounce and whirl around,
Toes on the ground.

Bounce and whirl around
One child says the rhyme, as she bounces the ball and turns around to catch it. She counts how many times she can do this without missing, trying to beat the previous score.

Syria

Ichi, ni, san
The children hold up their fingers to match each number, as they sing or say the rhyme.

Music – P42-43

Japan

With my hands
The children play by themselves or in a group, fitting the actions to the rhyme or song.

Music – P42-43

Australia, UK, USA

One – ichi, two – ni, three – san,
Two then four then five,
Three one two then four,
Then two, then four, then five.

With my hands I clap, clap, clap.
With my feet I tap, tap, tap.
Right foot first,
Left foot, then
Turn around and back again.

One – uno,
Two – dos,
Three – tres,
THROW!

One – muoy,
Two – pi,
Three – bey,
JUMP!

Here I come
With one leg.
Watch me run,
I'll catch YOU.

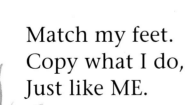

Match my feet.
Copy what I do,
Just like ME.

Uno, dos, tres
Stretch a string between two objects and mark a line a metre away. Children stand behind the line and take turns to throw bean bags at the string. Any child who hits it, scores a point.
Chile

Muoy, pi, bey
Trace two parallel lines in the soil, a short distance apart. The children say the rhyme and on "JUMP!" each child in turn jumps from the starting line to the far side of the second line. Any child who cannot jump the distance is out. The second line is then moved a little further away. The game continues until one child is left.
Cambodia

Here I come
The catcher stands in a circle of chalk. Children hop in and out of the circle. When a player is inside the circle, the catcher can tag him using his foot. The first child caught becomes the new catcher.
Thailand

Match my feet
The children stand in a circle. One child, the Star, claps a rhythm and everyone joins in, then she stands in front of another child and makes up a dance to the rhythm. If the second child can copy the dance, he becomes the Star. If not, the Star chooses a different child and repeats the dance.
Zaire

Catch You Games

Fire on the mountain

The children lie face-up, outside a safe area known as 'home'. The leader pretends to look far away for fire. He says "Fire on the mountain" and the children repeat "Fire, fire". He then says "Fire in the valley" and the children chorus "Fire, fire". He continues naming places where he can see fire, until he says "Fire right HERE". The children jump up and run for home. The last one home is out of the game.

Tanzania

Grandmother, what do you want?

The children stand behind a starting line opposite Grandmother, who can have her face or back to them, depending on the children's age. The first child asks Grandmother, "What do you want?". She replies any of the following: "2 giant strides", "4 mouse steps", "3 fairy feet", etc. The child carries out the steps, then it is the next child's turn. The child who gets close enough to Grandmother to touch her is the winner, and becomes the new Grandmother.

Belgium, Switzerland

Fire on the mountain,
Fire, fire,
Fire in the valley,
Fire, fire,
Fire right HERE.

MHLANGU AND
DAUGHTERS
GENERAL STORE

Grandmother,
What do you want?
Que veux-tu?

Un, deux, trois, quatre

Four children stand, one in each corner of an imaginary square, with a fifth in the middle. On "ALL CHANGE!", the children at the corners swop places, while the child in the middle tries to get into an empty corner first.

France, UK

Socorro!

A chaser runs after the children and tries to catch them. When a child is in danger of being caught, she shouts "Socorro!" If a player comes and holds her hand, they are both safe from being caught. Once the danger is past, they continue playing by themselves.

Peru

Taia ya taia!

The catcher shouts "Taia ya taia" and starts hopping on one foot. The other players chase him and try to tag him. As they do, he tries to tag them. Any player he touches becomes the new catcher.

Egypt

Uno, due, tre, STELLA

The leader turns her back. The other children creep up, trying to touch her. She counts "one, two, three" and on "STELLA" turns round. Any child she sees moving has to go back to the starting line. The first child to touch her back becomes the leader.

France, Italy

One – un,
Two – deux,
Three – trois,
Four – quatre,
ALL CHANGE!

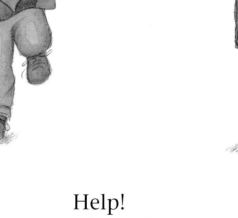

Help!
Socorro!
Help me
QUICK!

Taia ya
Taia!
Tag me
If you can!

One – uno,
Two – due,
Three – tre,
STELLA.

Ball Games

Queenie, Queenie

One child is chosen to be Queenie. She stands with her back to the other children and throws the ball over her head towards them. The child who picks it up hides it behind her back, and everyone says the rhyme. Queenie then turns round and guesses who has the ball. If she picks the right child, he becomes the new Queenie.

UK

Hot potato

The children sit in a circle. A bean bag or soft ball is passed round as quickly as possible, while they chant "hot potato". When the leader shouts "OUT!", the child who is holding the ball is out.

Ireland, UK, USA

Queenie, Queenie,
Who's got the ball?
Is she tall or is she small,
Is she fat or is she thin,
Or does she have a double chin?

Hot potato,
Hot potato,
Hot potato,
OUT!

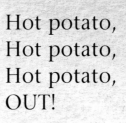

Clap, clap, clap

The children stand in two rows, a distance apart. The first child throws the ball to someone in the other row. As he throws, all the players clap; when the ball is caught they all stamp their feet. The catcher then throws the ball back to another child. The clapping and stamping continues as the ball is thrown from one row to the other. If anyone drops the ball, it is returned to the thrower, and the game continues until the children are tired.

Cameroon

One, two, three a-leerie

Children can play alone or in a group. On the numbers in the rhyme, the child bounces the ball. On "a-leerie" she lifts one leg over the ball, then catches it. On "catch me" she bounces the ball, twirls around and catches it.

UK

Pig in the middle

Three children make a line, and the central one is the Pig in the Middle (or any other animal you choose). The two end children throw or roll the ball to each other, saying the first two lines, and the Pig says "Yes, I CAN!" as he tries to catch it. If the Pig gets the ball he changes places with the child who threw it.

Ireland, UK

Clap, clap, clap,
Catch the ball.
Stamp, stamp, stamp,
Who's caught the ball?

One, two, three a-leerie,
Four, five, six a-leerie,
Seven, eight, nine a-leerie,
Ten a-leerie,
Catch me.

Pig in the middle,
Can't get out.
Yes, I CAN!

Hide and Seek Games

Eins, zwei, drei
One child is chosen to hide. After counting to five, the rest of the children go off to search. The child who finds the hidden child hides next time.

Germany, UK

Jack, Jack, shine your light
One child is chosen to be Jack, and goes off with a torch anywhere in the house. The others call out the rhyme and he shines his torch in reply, once. The others try to find him, but he keeps moving. They repeat the rhyme and he shows his light from his new hiding place, and then moves again. The child who catches him becomes Jack.

UK

One – eins
Two – zwei
Three – drei
Four – vier
Five – fünf
We're COMING!

Jack, Jack, shine your light,
Aren't you playing out tonight?

One, two, three ... WHOOP!

One child hides his eyes and counts to ten, while the others hide. When they are all hidden they shout "WHOOP!". The seeker tries to find them and catch them; meanwhile they try to run 'home' without being seen. The first one caught becomes the new seeker.

UK

Sardines

All the players shut their eyes and say the rhyme while one child hides. As soon as a seeker finds the hiding child, he joins her in the hiding place. Play continues until all the players are squashed together in the same place, like sardines. The first child who found the hiding place, hides next time.

Australia, Canada, UK

Huckle, buckle, BEANSTALK!

One child hides a small object in full view. The other children hunt for it. As soon as they see it they say, "Huckle buckle beanstalk" and sit down without looking at it. The first child to sit down hides it the next time.

USA

One, two, three, four, five,
Six, seven, eight, nine, ten.
Are you ready?
WHOOP!

Sardines in a tin,
One more to fit in.
Pull, push, squeeze,
Move up PLEASE!

Huckle, buckle,
BEANSTALK!

Clap, Skip and Jump Games

My father went to sea

Two children face each other and clap hands together, trying not to make a mistake. Either make up your own clapping pattern, or use the following:

Lines 1-3: On alternate beats, clap right then left hands together, and on "sea, sea, sea" clap own hands together.

Line 4: Clap own hands on each beat.

Line 5: Clap each other's hands together on "SEA, SEA, SEA".

UK

A mosquito one

This is a counting game. The children slap the floor or clap on the word "mosquito". They hold up the correct number of fingers as the numbers are called out, making up actions for lines 2, 4, 6, 8 and 10.

Caribbean

My father went to sea, sea, sea,
To see what he could see, see, see.
But all that he could see, see, see,
Was the bottom of the deep blue
SEA, SEA, SEA.

A mosquito one, a mosquito two,
A mosquito jump in the old man shoe,
A mosquito three, a mosquito four,
A mosquito open the old man door.
A mosquito five, a mosquito six,
A mosquito pick up the old man sticks.
A mosquito seven, a mosquito eight,
A mosquito open the old man gate.
A mosquito nine, a mosquito ten,
A mosquito biting the man again.

Higher and higher,
Up it goes,
Where it stops
Nobody knows.

Bluebells, cockle shells,
Eevy, ivy, OVER.

Andy, Mandy,
Sugar Candy,
Now's the time
To MISS!

Pina-one,
Pina-two,
Pina-three,
PINAFORE.

Higher and higher
The children see who can jump the highest over a rope, chanting the rhyme at every jump. After each round, the rope is moved higher.

Morocco, UK, USA

Bluebells, cockle shells
The aim is to jump the most 'overs'. Two children sway the rope from side to side as the children jump over it. When the rhyme says "over", they turn the rope full circle and continue turning faster and faster until someone trips.

UK

Andy, mandy, sugar candy
Two children turn the rope for the others. Just before "MISS!", they all run out. Anyone caught by the rope becomes a rope turner, or misses a turn.

UK, USA

Pina-one
The children see who can skip four skips without tripping – one on each beat of the rhyme.

Belgium, UK

Singing Games

Tootsie in da moonlight

The children stand in a circle, clapping as they sing. One child is chosen to be Tootsie, and walks around the outside of the circle as the others clap and point at her. On "Walk in", Tootsie walks into the middle, and stands and waits. Tootsie sings verse three, and as she says the name of a child in the group, this child joins Tootsie in the circle. They join hands and skip while the circle sings "Tra la la". Then the chosen child becomes the new Tootsie, and the game begins again.

Music – P42-43

Caribbean

Tootsie in da moonlight,
Tootsie in da dew,
Tootsie never come back
Before the clock struck two.

Walk in, Tootsie, walk in,
Walk right in I say.
Walk into my parlour
To hear my banjo play.

I don't love nobody
And nobody loves me.
All I love is Mary
To come and dance with me.

Tra la la la la la la,
Tra la la la la,
Tra la la la la la la,
Tra la la la la.

Che-che-koo-lay,
Che-che-koo-lay,
Che-che ko-fi sa,
Che-che ko-fi sa,
Ko-fi sa-lan-ga,
Ko-fi sa-lan-ga,
Ca-ca-shi lan-ga,
Ca-ca-shi lan-ga,
Koom a-day-day,
Koom a-day-day.

In and out of the Dusty Bluebells,
In and out of the Dusty Bluebells,
In and out of the Dusty Bluebells,
Who shall be my darling?

Pitter, patter, pitter, patter on
   your shoulders,
Pitter, patter, pitter, patter on
   your shoulders,
Pitter, patter, pitter, patter on
   your shoulders,
You shall be my darling.

Che-che-Koo-lay

The children form a circle with one child in the middle who sings the 1st line with hands on his head. The other children copy the action. On the 3rd line he touches his shoulders, on the 5th line his hips and on the 7th line his ankles. Each time the other children copy him. On "Koom a-day-day" they all fall down and lie there until the child in the middle jumps up. The other children then run away and the child who is caught is the next 'It'.

Music – P42-43

Ghana

The Dusty Bluebells

The children form a circle. Holding hands, they raise their arms to make arches. One child skips in and out of the arches, singing. At the end of the first verse she stops in front of the nearest child and pats him on alternate shoulders as she sings the second verse. That child then becomes the leader and the first child holds onto his waist as they skip under the arches.

Music – P42-43

UK

Music

The following rhymes can either be said, or sung. If you want to sing or hum them, try these easy tunes.

Ichi, ni, san

See page 19

One, two, three, Two then four then five,
Ichi, ni, san,

Three one two then four, Then two, then four, then five.

With my hands

See page 19

With my hands I clap, clap, clap. With my feet I tap, tap, tap.

Right foot first, Left foot, then Turn a-round and back a-gain.

Tootsie in da moonlight

See page 38

Toot - sie in da moon - light, Toot - sie in da dew,

Toot - sie ne - ver come back be - fore the clock struck two.

Che-che-koo-lay

See page 40

Che-che-koo-lay, Che-che-koo-lay, Che-che ko-fi sa, Che-che ko-fi sa,

Ko-fi sa-lan-ga, Ko-fi sa-lan-ga, Ca-ca-shi lan-ga, Ca-ca-shi lan-ga,

Koom a-day-day, Koom a-day-day.

The Dusty Bluebells

See page 41

In and out of the Dus-ty Blue-bells, In and out of the Dus-ty Blue-bells,

In and out of the Dus-ty Blue-bells, Who shall be my dar - ling?

Verse 2 begins :

Pit-ter pat-ter pit-ter pat-ter

10 tips to help you run the games

1. The first time you play a game, simplify it and speak slowly, taking part as both organiser and player. This way, children can learn from watching as well as listening.

2. End a game by summing up and giving some praise for effort. Try to replay the same game straightaway, as children like a second chance to improve their play.

3. Each time you play a game, follow the same routine, so children can put all their concentration into getting better at it.

4. Children need new challenges so, as they develop skills, introduce new games or add more complicated rules to games they already know.

5. If children are reluctant to join in, coax them to do so, and when they do, make sure they have fun. With luck, they'll want to play next time!

6. In games where children are eliminated, make sure that when they are out they don't get bored. Have a special task for them to do or ask them to help you run the game.

7. Look for extra opportunities to talk to children whilst you play. Try giving a running commentary on how the game is going and what someone is doing!

8. As children get to know a game well, they may be capable of running it themselves. Stay around at first, as they may need a little help from you.

9. Success is vital for motivation. Encourage and be positive: negative remarks are not constructive and can break bonds. Praise participation, effort and achievement as well as actual winning, but remember children are critical of unjustified praise!

10. Games are about having fun, and you can put a lot of fun into them. Add suspense by the way you use your voice and your actions. Be playful, and sometimes more daring than the children expect. It all adds to everyone's enjoyment.

Index of Games

A mosquito one 35

Acker backa boo! 15

Andar, Bahar 10

Andy, mandy, sugar candy 37

Bluebells, cockle shells 36

Bounce and whirl around 18

Che-che-koo-lay 40

Clap, clap, clap 28

Cross your hands 13

The Dusty Bluebells 41

Eins, zwei, drei 30

Fire on the mountain 22

Grandmother, what do you want? 23

Here I come 21

Higher and higher 36

Hot potato 27

Huckle, buckle, BEANSTALK! 33

Hum a dum dum 13

I looked high 12

Ichi, ni, san 19

Jack, Jack, shine your light 31

Match my feet 21

Muoy, pi, bey 20

My father went to sea 34

Olika bolika 15

One, two, three a-leerie 29

One, two, three ... WHOOP! 32

Pig in the middle 29

Pina-one 37

Queenie, Queenie 26

Ram, ram, RIP 17

Sardines 33

Socorro! 24

Stroke the baby 12

Taia ya taia! 25

Tickum-tackum 16

Tootsie in da moonlight 38

Un, deux, trois, quatre 24

Uno, dos, tres 20

Uno, due, tre, STELLA 25

Up and down 17

With my hands 19

Wolf, Wolf, where are you? 10

These games are known to be played in the following countries:

Australia, Belgium, Cambodia, Cameroon, Canada, Caribbean, Chile, Egypt, France, Germany, Ghana, Holland, India, Indonesia, Iran, Ireland, Italy, Japan, Malaysia, Morocco, Pakistan, Peru, Sri Lanka, Switzerland, Syria, Tanzania, Thailand, UK, USA, Zaire.

They may also be played in other countries around the world.